SCHOOL OF SYSTEMATIC THEOLOGY

BOOK 2

"GOD'S GIFT TO MAN"

The Doctrines of Man, Sin, and Salvation

A ministry of:

Striving For Eternity Ministries

SCHOOL OF SYSTEMATIC THEOLOGY

BOOK 2

"GOD'S GIFT TO MAN"

The Doctrines of Man, Sin, and Salvation

A ministry of:

Striving For Eternity Ministries

School of Systematic Theology Book 2

"God's Gift to Man"

THE DOCTRINE OF MAN

    Lesson 1 - The Creation of Man

    Lesson 2 - The Constitution of Man

THE DOCTRINE OF SIN

    Lesson 3 - The Identification of Sin

    Lesson 4 - The Initiation of Sin

THE DOCTRINE OF SALVATION

    Lesson 5 - The Father and Salvation

    Lesson 6 - Christ and Salvation

    Lesson 7 - The Spirit and Salvation

    Lesson 8 – God's Sovereignty and Man's Responsibility

    Lesson 9 - Eternal Security

    Lesson 10 - The Blessings of Salvation

Bibliography

A Ministry of:

Striving For Eternities Ministries
www.StrivingForEternity.org

SECTION I:

THE DOCTRINE OF MAN

Lesson 1:
The Creation of Man

The doctrine of man, also called _____ is a study of the origin of man. In the studies on the doctrine of man we will examine the creation of man as well as the constitution of man.

In studying the creation man we need to answer two important questions: how was man created and how is man procreated.

I. THE ORIGINAL CREATION OF MAN

In studying the original creation of man we need to first address the false views of how man was originally created and then examine the biblical account of man's original creation.

A. *False Views*

1. _____

   a) **Explained**
   Man descended from the lower animals, body and soul, by a perfectly natural process, controlled entirely by inherent forces.

   b) **Refuted**
   Apart from addressing all the beliefs of the evolutionists there are four basic problems with evolution.

   1) *There is no evidence that evolution is still _____.*

   2) *The science of _____ proves that the theory of evolution is impossible. The idea of simple developing into more complex creatures cannot happen, for science shows that the DNA can only lose information not gain it.*

   3) *The lack of _____ forms is something unexplainable for evolutionist.*

4) Their basis for evolution is the _____ _____ which has been grossly misinterpreted.

5) No answer for _____. Chemicals do not develop an ethical system of right and wrong.

It must be understood that evolution is a _____ and not a scientific fact. From the Christians standpoint, the primary problem with evolution is that it undermines the integrity of the Bible and specifically the creation account of Genesis chapter one.

2. _____ _____

   a) **Explained**
   This view claims to acknowledge the fact that _____ is the ultimate Creator, but believes that God used _____ processes in the work of creation.

   b) **Refuted**
   The primary problem with this view is that its subscribers claim to believe in God, yet reject the biblical account of creation in six literal days. They make human reasoning superior to the authority of Scripture.

   c) **Significant**
   In Genesis chapter one the word "day" is a literal 24-hour day, thus making creation of man on the sixth literal day of creation.

   (1) This word "day" (yom) used with numbers always means 24-hour day.

   (2) The phase "evening-morning" emphasize literal day.

   (3) Sabbath observance based on literal days (Exodus 20:11).

B. Biblical View

1. **Concerning *Man***

   a) **Statement**
   The first man was created _____ and _____.

   b) **Scriptures**

   (1) *Genesis 1:26-27*

   (2) *Genesis 2:7*

   (3) *Matthew 19:4*

2. **Concerning Woman**

   a) **Statement**
   The woman was created _____ in Adam and then brought into being through a special creative act.

   b) **Scriptures**

   (1) *Genesis 1:27*

   (2) *Genesis 2:22*

   (3) *Matthew 19:4*

   (4) *1 Timothy 2:15*

The first man and woman were created directly and uniquely by God. The question now comes as to the ongoing creation of man.

II. THE ONGOING CREATION OF MAN

This topic is very important because it is at the heart of the current issue of _____.

There are basically three theories which are taught concerning the ongoing creation, or _____ of mankind.

A. The _____ Theory

1. Definition

This view believes that man's soul exists _____ to the conception and is united with the baby at birth.

2. Refutation

a) This view has no support; it is founded in _____.

b) God created Adam's soul as well as his body (Genesis 2:7)

c) Children exhibit characteristics of their parents.

3. Question

Can a person hold to this view of the soul and conception and still believe in abortion?

B. The _____ Theory

1. Definition

This view believes that each soul is _____ created by God and joined to the body either at conception or birth.

2. Refutation

The primary problem with this view is that it makes God the author of _____ in the creation of the sinful nature of each person.

3. Question

Can a person hold to this view of the soul and conception and still believe in abortion?

C. The _____ Theory

1. Definition

The entire human race was _____ created in Adam. All individuals are entirely _____, body and soul/spirit.

2. Explanation

- a) This makes a fetus a human at _____ (Exodus 21:22-24).

- b) Only once is the "breath of life" breathed into man, which made him a living soul (Genesis 2:7; 5:3-32).

- c) The Scriptures teaches that the entire human is produced by procreation (Genesis 5:3; 1 Corinthians 11:8-12)

- d) God knew men as distinct persons _____ their physical birth

    - (1) *Jeremiah 1:5 -*
    - (2) *Psalm 139:13-15 -*
    - (3) *Luke 1:41 -*
    - (4) *Galatians 1:15 -*

- e) This view allows for the teaching of Scripture that "all men sinned in Adam" (Romans 5:12).

3. **Question**

Can a person hold to this view of the soul and conception and still believe in abortion?

THOUGHT QUESTIONS FOR LESSON 1

1. A friend of yours at college maintains that evolution is a proven fact. Without getting into the scientific evidences, what problems would you remind this person of concerning evolution?

2. One of your Christian neighbors tells you she was taught that God actually used evolution to create mankind. How would you help this dear sister?

3. A co-worker you have talked to about abortion seems to think that God creates each person at birth and not at conception. Assuming he will accept God's authority, what truths and Scriptures would you show this person?

www.StrivingForEternity.org

Lesson 2:
The Constitution of Man

This lesson focuses on the makeup or constitution of man. Is he just a physical body as the evolutionists would like us to think, or is his constitution more than that? "How did God _____ man?"

We will examine the Scriptures and see how they describe for us the design of man.

I. MAN WAS CREATED IN THE IMAGE OF GOD

A. The Meaning of "The Image of God"

1. **Refers to Man's likeness to God as a _____**
   This includes the fact that man, like God, possesses:

   a) Self-Consciousness

   b) God-Consciousness

   c) Intellect

   d) Emotion

   e) Will

   f) Creativity

2. **Refers to Man's likeness to God as a _____**
   It is man's likeness to God as a spirit which enables him to _____ God.

3. **Refers to Man's likeness to God as a _____ being**

   a) Man's moral nature includes his ability to _____ right from wrong as well as the ability to _____ in accord to these standards (Romans 2:14).

   b) This aspect of the image of God involves the existence of a _____ in man (Romans 2:14-16).

   c) The conscience of man at the fall was _____ but not _____ (Genesis 9:6; James 3:9)

B. The Significance of the "Image of God"

1. This means that each person is a _____ individual, whose life is precious to God and worthy of protection.

2. Having the image of God, though marred, makes redemption possible.

II. MAN WAS CREATED A PHYSICAL BEING

A. The Definition "body"
The body is the physical vessel in which the _____ resides. It is the vehicle of the _____.

B. The Description

1. The body was an essential part of the creation of man, considered _____ _____ by God at Creation (Genesis 1:31; 2:7).

2. Our earthly bodies should be considered part of our present _____ and are not to be held in contempt (1 Corinthians 6:19-20; 3 John 2).

3. A physical body will be part of the _____ state (1 Corinthians 15:54).

III. MAN WAS CREATED A SPIRITUAL BEING

Man is also a spiritual being. By spiritual we mean he possesses not only a physical nature but an _____ nature as well.

There are a number of words used to describe this aspect of man in Scripture.

A. Soul

1. **Its Old Testament Meaning (Nephesh)**
   The basic meaning of the Hebrew Word for Soul is _____. Since it is used in a general way, it may refer to:

   a) Living beings (Genesis 2:7; 1:20-21, 24, 30)

   b) That which departs from a body (Genesis 35:18)

   c) The body itself (Leviticus 13:2-3; Numbers 6:6)

School of Systematic Theology

        d)   The center of the emotional experiences

              1)   *Sympathy (Job 30:25)*

              2)   *Despair (Psalm 43:5)*

              3)   *Bitterness (2 Kings 4:27)*

              4)   *Hate (2 Samuel 5:8)*

              5)   *Love (Song of Solomon 1:7)*

              6)   *Grief (Jeremiah 13:17)*

    2.   **Its New Testament Meaning (Psyche)**

        a)   The soul may refer to the _____ person (Acts 2:41; 27:37).

        b)   This word for soul may refer to the _____ part of man (Matthew 10:28).

        c)   The word soul also designates those who are in the _____ state (Revelation 6:9).

B.   **Spirit**

This word strictly refers to the immaterial part of man. Man is a _____, but he cannot be said to be a spirit – he has a _____ (Ryrie).

Because the spirit of man relates to his immaterial facet, there are a number of ways in Scripture this is expressed.

    1.   **Grief (Genesis 26:35)**

    2.   **Jealousy (Number 5:14)**

    3.   **Contriteness (Psalm 34:18)**

    4.   **Remembering (Psalm 77:6)**

    5.   **Haughtiness (Proverbs 16:18)**

    6.   **Thinking (Isaiah 29:24)**

    7.   **Humility (Matthew 5:3)**

8. Vexation (John 13:21)

Since the spirit can produce undesirable traits, attention must be given to the spiritual life (Psalm 51; 2 Corinthians 7:1).

C. **Conscience**

1. The conscience is that part of man which _____ him to do what he thinks is right or not do what he thinks is wrong.

2. For the unsaved the conscience is not completely reliable (Acts 23:1; 1 Timothy 4:2; Titus 1:15; Romans 2:15).

3. For the saved, the conscience prods him to do what is right concerning:

   a) Obedience to government (Romans 13:5)

   b) Submission to unjust employers (1 Peter 2:19)

   c) Respect the conscience of a weaker brother or sister in Christ (1 Corinthians 8:7, 10, 12)

   d) Testify toward spiritual activity (Romans 9:1-2; 2 Corinthians 1:12; 4:2)

D. **Mind**

Throughout Scripture there is a clear distinction between the unsaved mind and the saved mind. The mind is the concept behind the Old Testament idea of _____.

1. The Unsaved Mind

   a) Reprobate (Romans 1:28)

   b) Blinded (2 Corinthians 4:4)

   c) Vain (Ephesians 4:17)

   d) Darkened (Ephesians 4:18)

   e) Defiled (Titus 1:15)

2. The Saved Mind

The believer's mind is the central place of _____ _____.

- a) The mind is to understand truth (Luke 24:45)
- b) The mind is renewed in a dedicated Christian (Romans 12:1-2).
- c) The mind discerns doubtful things (Romans 14:5)
- d) The mind pursues holiness (1 Peter 1:13)
- e) The mind understands the Lord's will (Ephesians 5:17)

E. Flesh

While this phrase often refers to the physical body, it is also used to describe that immaterial aspect within man which _____ God, called the sin nature (Romans 7:18; 1 Corinthians 3:3; 2 Corinthians 1:12; Galatians 5:17; Colossians 2:18; 2 Peter 2:10).

F. Heart

The heart in both the Old Testament and the New Testament expressed an individual's _____ of _____. We see as the seat in many aspects of Scripture.

1. The Heart is the seat of _____ life (Deuteronomy 8:5; Ps.119:11; Mat.15:19-20)

2. The Heart is the seat of _____ life (Deuteronomy 6:5; Job 27:6; Nehemiah 2:2; Psalm 37:4)

3. The Heart is the seat of _____ life (Exodus 14:5; 8:15; Hebrews 4:7)

4. The Heart is the seat of _____ life (Romans 10:9-10; 1 Peter 3:15; 1 Timothy 1:5)

THOUGHT QUESTIONS FOR LESSON 2

1. You read in a college textbook on psychology that there is no such thing as a soul. How would you define "psychology" according to Scripture?

2. Is the conscience a good guide for our morality of life? Why or why not?

3. Give some examples as how the conscience may work for the Christian in these texts:

    1) Romans 13:5 -

    2) 1 Peter 2:19 -

    3) Romans 9:1-2 -

    4) 1 Corinthians 8:7 -

4. Is there a difference between the soul and the spirit of man, and if so what is it? Does your answer mean that man is more than two facets?

5. Is there a difference between the heart and the mind in Scripture. What is the significance of your answer?

SECTION II:

THE DOCTRINE OF SIN

Lesson 3:
The Identification of Sin

Having studied the creation and constitution of man, we need to examine another doctrine also closely connected to the doctrine of salvation, and that is the doctrine of sin.

In these next two lessons we will examine what the Scriptures say concerning the identification of sin (what it is) and the initiation of sin (how it came into being).

In our pursuit toward identifying what sin is, we will examine an understanding of sin and the words used to describe sin.

I. A BIBLICAL UNDERSTANDING OF SIN

In seeking an understanding of sin, we need to first identify the incorrect understanding of sin and then present a correct understanding of sin.

A. Incorrect Understanding for Sin

4. **Sin is _____**
   This view equates sin with the _____ aspects of sin alone, and not with the heart issue.

5. **Sin is _____**
   This view sees sin as a failure to realize one's human _____.

6. **Sin is lack of _____ _____**
   This view regards sin as a result of the lack of God- consciousness as a person understands God.

7. **Sin is a _____ _____**
   This view sees sin as a result of their social disadvantages.

D. Correct Understanding of Sin

1. **Sin fundamentally involves an _____ of unbelief (Romans 8:7; Hebrews 3:12).**

2. **Sin involves _____ of lawlessness (1 John 3:4; Matthew 7:23).**
   Thus, sin is the lack of conformity to the moral law of God either in _____, _____, or _____.

II. THE BIBLICAL TERMS FOR SIN

(This section on biblical terms is primarily adapted from Basic Theology by Charles

Ryrie).

E. Terms in the Old Testament

1. Chata

a) Basic Meaning
"To _____ the _____"

b) Biblical Significance
Sin is missing the right mark and hitting the wrong mark. It is used in reference to moral evil, idolatry, and ceremonial sin.

c) Biblical References
Exodus 20:20; Judges 20:16; Proverbs 8:36; 19:2

2. Ra (Rasha)

a) Basic Meaning
"breaking up or _____"

b) Biblical Significance
This word is often used to refer to calamity, injurious things, or things morally wrong (often translated "wicked").

c) Biblical References
Genesis 3:5; 38:7; Judges 11:27

Also note use of word in Isaiah 45:7 as it refers to calamity and ruin.

3. Pasha

a) Basic Meaning
"to _____"

b) Biblical Significance
While the basic meaning is to rebel, it is often translated _____ which indicates a willing crossing of a boundary.

c) Biblical References
Exodus 34:7; Isaiah 1:2

4. Awah

a) Basic Meaning
"To be _____ or _____" (Note Isaiah 21:3 for literal use).

b) Biblical Significance
This term sees sin as perverseness. It is often translated _____.

c) Biblical References
Numbers 15:30-31; Isaiah 19:14

5. Shagag

a) Basic Meaning
"To ____ _____"

b) Biblical Significance
The significance of this word is that it indicates away from what one knows is right (i.e. God's moral law).

c) Biblical References
Leviticus 4:2; Numbers 15:22

F. Terms in the New Testament

1. Kakos

a) Basic Meaning
"Badness, either _____ or _____"

b) Biblical Significance
This is a very general term for sin in the New Testament.

c) Biblical References
Romans 12:17; 1 Timothy 6:10

2. Poneros

a) Basic Meaning
"Evil"

b) Biblical Significance
This is a term which almost exclusive means moral evil. It is used of Satan and demons.

c) Biblical References
John 17:15; Acts 19:12; 1 Thessalonians 5:22

3. Hamartia

a) Basic Meaning
"To _____ the _____"

b) Biblical Significance
Corresponding to the Hebrew word Chata, this is the most used word for sin in the New Testament (227 times).

c) Biblical References
Acts 2:38; Romans 5:12

4. Adikia

a) Basic Meaning
"The opposite of _____"

b) Biblical Significance
Used in reference to unrighteousness of any kind, refers to:

(1) *The Unsaved (Romans 1:18)*

(2) *Money (Luke 16:9)*

(3) *Actions (2 Thessalonians 2:10)*

5. Anomos

a) Basic Meaning
"The opposite of _____"

b) Biblical Significance
This term describes sin as lawlessness. Often translated "iniquity".

c) Biblical References
Matthew 13:41; 1 Timothy 1:9

6. **Parabates**

   a) **Basic Meaning**
   "To _____ against"

   b) **Biblical Significance**
   This term is usually associated with specific violations of the law.

   c) **Biblical References**
   Galatians 3:19; Hebrews 9:15

7. **Planao**

   a) **Basic Meaning**
   "To ____ _____"

   b) **Biblical Significance**
   To either deceive others (Matthew 24:5-6) or to deceive oneself (1 John 1:8).

8. **Paraptoma**

   a) **Basic Meaning**
   "to _____ _____"

   b) **Biblical Significance**
   This term defines sin as a deliberate falling away from truth.

   c) **Biblical References**
   Galatians 6:1; James 5:19

9. **Hypocrisis**

   a) **Basic Meaning**
   "To _____ as an _____"

   b) **Biblical Significance**
   The significance of this word is the deceitful nature of sin (false teachers, etc.).

   c) **Biblical References**
   1 Timothy 4:2

THOUGHT QUESTIONS FOR LESSON 3

1. While witnessing to someone, they tell you they do not commit acts of sin. What truth would you share with this person?

2. A Christian friend of yours just read Isaiah 45:7. After reading it they were confused with the fact that God created evil, knowing James 1:13 says he cannot tempt anyone with evil. How would you explain this text?

3. From the study above, compile a list of some other words beside "sin" to describe the concept of sin.

4. An individual says to you that they do not think sin is a very significant theme of Scripture. Without giving details, what truth may you want to supply this person?

Lesson 4:
The Initiation of Sin

Having examined what sin is in the previous lesson, this section will deal with the initiation of sin, or how sin came into the world.

The question is often asked: Why would God allow sin to enter into a perfect creation? While there are no Scriptures which answers this issue directly, it appears that the _____ to sin is part of creation.

I. SIN'S INITIATION INTO THE UNIVERSE - Satan

    A. *God is NOT the Initiator of Sin*

        10. There is no _____ in God (Deuteronomy 32:4)

        11. God cannot do _____ (Job 34:10)

        12. God _____ the workers of iniquity (Psalm 5:5; 7:11)

        13. God created man _____ and _____ (Ecclesiastes 7:29)

        14. God is _____ (Isaiah 6:3)

    G. *Satan IS the Initiator of Sin*

        1. **The Scriptures**

            a) Isaiah 14:14-17

            While this context does describe a historical figure, it is also clear that it is describing something beyond or behind that historical figure as well (cf. Eze.28:11-19; Isaiah 7:14, etc.).

            In this text we have the FIVE "I WILL'S" of Satan (Isaiah 14:13-14).

                1) **I will** ascend to heaven

                2) **I will** raise my throne above the stars of God

                3) **I will** sit on the mount of assembly

                4) **I will** ascend above the heights of the clouds

                5) **I will** make myself like the most High

b) Ezekiel 28:11-19

Here the power behind the King of Tyre is exposed by describing the rebellion of Satan, who is that power.

1) His Creation (vs. 28:12-15a)

(a) Wisdom (v. 12)

(b) Beauty (vs. 12-13)

(c) Position (v. 14)

(2) His Corruption (vs. 28:15b-19)

(3) His Condemnation (the SIX "I WILL'S" of YHWH)

a) **I will** cast thee as profane out of the mountain of God

b) **I will** destroy thee

c) **I will** cast thee to the ground

d) **I will** lay thee before kings, that they may behold you

e) **I will** bring forth a fire from the midst of thee, it shall devour thee

f) **I will** bring thee to ashes

2. The Significance

From these texts we may draw several conclusions:

a) Angels were created with the _____ to choose from moral alternatives.

b) A _____ to sin arose in Satan

c) The first sin was _____ against authority and _____ in his potential.

d) Satan is fully accountable for own sin. God did not _____ him, nor was he _____ in his creation. Sin was an act of his will.

II. SIN'S INITIATION INTO HUMANITY - Adam

Both man and woman were created in the image of God, yet fell by their own choosing. Notice these truths concerning Adam.

A. All of creation, including Adam was declared _____ by God (Genesis 1:31). Therefore, there was nothing in Adam's creation which programmed him to sin.

H. Temptation to Adam was _____, through Satan.

I. Adam's sin was _____, Eve was deceived (1 Timothy 2:14).

J. All of mankind has sinned in _____ (Romans 5:12).

III. SIN'S INITIATION INTO *THE INDIVIDUAL* - Depravity

A. The Entrance of Depravity

1. Since all of mankind sinned in Adam, each individual is born in a state of _____ (Romans 3:10-23; 5:12).

2. The passing of Adam's sin to the humanity is called the _____ of sin. The word *"imputation"* is a bookkeeping term which indicates *"God's calculation of your sin to your account"*.

B. The Explanation of Depravity

1. Depravity does NOT mean:

    a) That an unsaved individual has no disposition or tendency to do _____ (Romans 2:14).

    b) That an unsaved individual never does anything _____ (Matthew 23:23).

    c) That an unsaved individual is as _____ as they could possibly be (2 Timothy 3:13).

d) That an unsaved individual will indulge in every _____ of sin.

2. **Depravity DOES mean:**

a) Man is completely corrupted and controlled by sin (Titus 1:15; 2 Corinthians 7:1).

   (1) Body (Romans 8:10)

   (2) Mind (Titus 1:15; Romans 8:6)

   (3) Heart (Jeremiah 17:9)

   (4) Will (John 8:34)

b) By God's standard, there is no spiritual _____ in the sinner.

   (1) A sinner cannot do anything to please God (Isaiah 64:6; Proverbs 21:4).

   (2) A sinner cannot do anything to change his preference for sin (1 John 1:8-2:2).

c) There is no possible means of _____ within the depraved sinner (Roman 1:18; Ephesians 2:1, 8).

THOUGHT QUESTIONS FOR LESSON 4

1. Read Genesis 3:1-5. In what way is this text similar to Isaiah 14:14-17?

2. A young believer asks you how Satan could have desired to sin if God created him while declaring all His creation "good". How would you answer this honest question?

3. Describe in you own words what "depravity" is and provide two key Scriptures (try this without looking back at your notes).

4. An individual who is unclear about depravity is baffled that some unsaved people can be so nice. Help this person to reconcile this dilemma.

SECTION III:

THE DOCTRINE OF SALVATION

Lesson 5:
The Father and Salvation

In the Doctrine of Man we learned that man was created unique from the animal (Genesis 1:26-27) in the image of God. In the study of the Doctrine of Sin we learned that, because man sinned and is now by nature a sinner (Romans 3:10, 23), his soul is separated from God spiritually, and, without an act of God, separated for eternity (Revelation 20:11-15).

This leads us into the crucial study of the Doctrine of Salvation. The word "salvation" both in the Old Testament and the New Testament has the basic idea of "deliverance, to make safe and sound". In the Scriptures this term can refer to saving someone from:

1) Physical disease (Luke 18:42; Matthew 9:22)
2) Temporal danger (Matthew 8:25; Acts 27:20)
3) Eternal damnation (Matthew 1:21; Romans 5:9)

The focus of our study is salvation as it relates to the deliverance of the soul from eternal damnation.

We will begin our study of this doctrine by examine the work of the triune God in providing this wonderful salvation. There are three key texts which elaborate on the three persons of the Godhead all active in working out salvation in the life of the believer, **Ephesians 1:3-14, Titus 3:3-7 and 1 Peter 1:2**.

I. THE FATHER PLANNED SALVATION

A. *He is the Initiator*

1. The Scriptures

a) John 1:13
Man could not become a child of God by _____ it. It took an act of God to make that provision.

b) John 6:44 (12:32)
These verses teaches it is impossible for anyone on their own initiative to seek salvation or to know the true God. How does the Father draw men unto Himself?

1) The **Spirit** (1 Thessalonians 1:3-4; 2 Thessalonians 2:13)
2) The **Scriptures** (2 Thessalonians 2:13; 2 Timothy 3:15)
3) The **Servant** (Acts 1:8; Romans 10:14-15)

The Spirit _____ the sinner of their need.

The Scripture _____ to the sinner their need

The Servant is part of God's plan to _____ to the sinner.

2. The Significance

Because man is depraved, there is nothing within Him that _____ God. God therefore, needed to initiate His divine plan.

B. *He is the Designer (Ephesians 1:3-12; 1 Peter 1:2)*

It is God who designed the entire plan of salvation. The issue of God's election in salvation will be covered in Lesson 8.

1. His Promise (Genesis 3:15)

The moment that sin entered the human race and corrupted all of mankind, God promised to them the victory over sin and Satan. It would be in the _____ and would be the _____ of woman. This is a clear promise of the Messiah.

2. His Provisions

a) Grace

1) *Definition:*

Both the New Testament word (charis) and the Old Testament word (chen) have the concept of _____ _____.

2) *Explanation:*

In relation to salvation, "grace" may best be understood as "God's favor to sinners who:

do not _____ it,

cannot _____ it,

cannot _____ it and

do not _____ it.

So then "grace" is God's response of love to the plight of mankind which makes salvation _____ for all.

b) Sacrifice

1) *Planned before _____*

Before man fell into sin, God foreknew his plight and provided before time began the provision for men to be reconciled to God (Ephesians 1:4; Revelation 13:8).

2) Pictured in Old Testament _____

- a) The Day of Atonement (Leviticus 16)
- b) Passover (Exodus 12:3)
- c) Daily Sacrifices (Exodus 29:38-42)

3) Provided in Christ

Christ became that perfect lamb for the sacrifice of sin.

- a) John 1:29, 36
- b) 1 Peter 1:19
- c) Revelation 5:8
- d) Hebrews 9:14

(This topic will be covered more fully in the following lesson)

c) Revelation

1) 2 Timothy 3:14-17

It is the Scriptures, which were inspired by God, which are able to make a person _____ unto salvation.

2) 1 Thessalonians 1:4

The reason Paul was sure of his election was because the _____ came in power and in connection with the Holy Spirit.

d) The Holy Spirit

It is the Spirit of God who _____ of sin (John 16:7-8) and _____ the individual to the Father (John 6:44). The work of the Spirit in the salvation of an individual is discussed in Lesson 7.

THOUGHT QUESTION FOR LESSON 5

1. How does our understanding of the doctrine of man and the doctrine of sin effect our understanding of the doctrine of salvation?

2. A friend who you have been witnessing to tells you that they have been saved because God protected them in an accident. How would you answer your friend?

3. How does the Father "draw" a sinner to Himself?

   1)

   2)

   3)

4. What role does the Christian play in the Father drawing sinners unto Himself?

Lesson 6:
Christ and Salvation

Our study of the doctrine of salvation began by examining the work of the triune God in providing this wonderful salvation. There are three key texts which elaborate on the three persons of the Godhead all active in working out salvation in the life of the believer, **Ephesians 1:3-14, Titus 3:3-7 and 1 Peter 1:2**.

This lesson focuses on the work of Christ in our salvation. This answers the question, "Why did Christ have to die?"

I. THE FATHER PLANNED SALVATION (Lesson 5)

II. THE SON PROVIDED SALVATION

We see that Jesus Christ provided the _____ for our sin and thus a way to a relationship with the Father.

A. Christ's Death and His Suffering

The "Passion Week" of Christ is the last week of His earthly life in which His human suffering for sin reached its pinnacle.

1. His Examinations

a) At the House of Annas (John 18:12-13)
Because Annas was the Father-in-law of Caiaphas they brought Christ bound to Him first, then to Caiaphas.

b) In the Court of Caiaphas (Matthew 26:57-75; Mark 14:53-65)

(1) *Accused Him of _____ _____ (Matthew 26:61; see John 2:19)*

(2) *Accused Him of _____ (Matthew 26:63-65)*

It is also here that _____ sat in the inner courtyard of the palace and _____ Christ.

c) Before the Sanhedrin (Luke 22:66-71)
This was the Great council of the Jews consisting of 70-72 elders and teachers of the Jews. They asked Jesus if He was the _____. After hearing it, they led Him to

Pilate. The reason for this is they could not carry out their sentence, but present it to the Roman government.

- d) **Before Pilate (Luke 23:1-5; Matthew 27:11-14)**
  It was here Pilate asked whether Christ was the _____ of the Jews. The scribes and elders came with Him to accuse Him before Pilate, saying that Jesus was attempting to subvert Rome by claiming Himself a King and refusing to pay taxes. This made the issue _____.

  Having heard He was from Galilee, He sent Jesus to Herod.

- e) **Before Herod (Luke 23: 8-12)**
  Herod had heard of Jesus and wanted to see Him perform a miracle. Having the pressure of the elders and scribes accusing Him, he opted for making a _____ of this so called king with a purple robe and crown of thrones.

- f) **Back to Pilate (Luke 23:13-26)**
  It was during this examination that Pilate found Christ faultless and desired to release Him as the one allowed freedom at the feast. The crowd, spearheaded by the elders and scribes, cried out for His crucifixion. Pilate complied, washing His hands of the blood of Jesus.

2. **His Execution**

   a) **The Time of His Execution**
   He was executed on _____ morning and died prior to Sunset that same evening. By Jewish reckoning three days would have included Friday prior to sunset,

   Saturday is day two and then Sunday, day three, at daybreak is when He resurrected.

   b) **The Type of Execution**
   (From Ryrie, Basic Theology, p.284)

   "Crucifixion was eastern in origin. The Persians practiced it and Alexander the Great seemed to have learned it from them. Phoenicia, famed for its barbaric practices, frequently employed crucifixion. Rome apparently borrowed it from Carthage and perfected it as a means of capital punishment. The extent to which Rome used it staggers the imagination.

After being sentence, the condemned person was flogged with a leather whip loaded with metal or bone. He was then required to shoulder the cross beam and carry it to the place of execution. This beam was approximately six feet long and weighed about thirty pounds. This was affixed to the upright stake which was already in place at the execution sight. Nails about seven inches long with a head (to keep the body from sliding off) were driven through the hands and feet of the victim. Sometimes ropes were also used to keep the body on the cross.

The Romans had learned to push the feet upward when they nailed them to the cross so that the victim could lean on the nail and push himself upward momentarily in order to breathe easier. Death rarely came in less than thirty-six hours, though most people survived two or three days before they died. Insatiable thirst, pain from the scourging, cramps, dizziness, public shame, and the horror of know what lay head before the release of death, all combined to make crucifixion a horrible means of dying."

B. Christ's Death and its Significance

1. **Atonement**

   a) **Definition:**
   This is the fact that Jesus Christ became our _____ for sin, and has eternally satisfied our payment for sin.

   b) **Scriptures:**
   Leviticus 16; 1 Peter 3:18; 2 Corinthians 5:21

2. **Redemption**

   a) **Definition:**
   _____ because of a payment made (Ryrie, p. 290). In this case the payment was the death of Christ.

   b) **Old Testament Words:**

   (1) *g'l*
   This word is related to the idea of the _____ _____, which was the price of the family obligation (Ruth 4:6).

(2) pdh
The paying of a _____ without family obligation (Exodus 13:12; Numbers 18:15-17).

> *¹² that you shall set apart to the Lord all that open the womb, that is, every firstborn that comes from an animal which you have; the males shall be the Lord's.* (Exodus 13:12)

(3) kopher
The sum paid to redeem a _____ life (Exodus 21:28; 30:12).

c) New Testament Words

(1) Agorazo
The idea of _____ in the marketplace.

This teaches:
1) Who paid the price (2 Peter 2:1);
2) What was the price (Revelation 5:9-10);
3) What was bought and who owns it (1 Corinthians 6:19-20)

(2) Peripoiumai
This word means to keep safe or purchase for one's self (Acts 20:28).

(3) Lutroo
Literally means to loosen, as a trapped animal or prisoner. Thus a release on receipt of ransom (Titus 2:14; 1 Peter 1:18-19).

3. Reconciliation

a) Definition
Altering a relation from one of _____ to one of _____.

b) Need
It is because man is in a condition of _____ that the need for reconciliation is real (Psalm 5:4-5; Romans 5:9-10).

c) **Scriptures**

   (1) *2 Corinthians 5:18-20 –*

   (2) *Romans 5:10*

4. **Propitiation**

   a) **Propitiation**
   Because of the reality of the wrath of God, an _____ is necessary to appease that wrath.

   b) **Wrath**
   There are twenty different words used almost 600 times in the Old Testament to describe the wrath of God against sin. God, however, is never unreasonable. His wrath is always righteous, and His grace allows for ways to have fellowship with Him.

   While the New Testament does not speak as much on God's wrath, the reality of it is still present in two Greek words ORGE and thumos (John 3:36; Romans 1:18; Ephesians 2:3; 1 Thessalonians 2:16; Revelation 6:16; 14:10; 16:1; 19:15).

   c) **Offering**
   The offering of appeasement for the wrath of God was clearly the _____ of Christ (Romans 3:25; 1 John 2:2; Hebrews 2:17).

THOUGHT QUESTION FOR LESSON 6

1. What are some of the practical benefits in being fully acquainted with the suffering of Christ?

2. Concerning the offering of Christ, which provided the offering of salvation, His death or His blood? Explain your answer.

3. Explain in your own words the meanings and distinctions between these four words. What does each have to with salvation? How does the work of Christ effect each?

   1) Atonement

   2) Redemption

   3) Reconciliation

   4) Propitiation

Lesson 7:
The Spirit and Salvation

Our study of the doctrine of salvation began by examining the work of the triune God in providing this wonderful salvation. There are three key texts which elaborate on the three persons of the Godhead all active in working out salvation in the life of the believer, **Ephesians 1:3-14, Titus 3:3-7 and 1 Peter 1:2**.

This lesson will focus on the work of the Spirit in Salvation, particularly how the Spirit _____ salvation.

I. THE FATHER PLANNED SALVATION (Lesson 5)

II. THE SON PROVIDED SALVATION (Lesson 6)

III. THE SPIRIT PERFORMED SALVATION

There are four main works of the Spirit of God in relation to the application of salvation.

A. Conviction

1. Definition

This is the work of the Spirit which is internally convincing mankind of their _____ of salvation.

The convicting work of the Spirit occurs prior to actual salvation. Not everyone who is convicted of sin repents of their sin.

2. Scripture

a) **Promise of His Ministry (John 16:8-12)**

In this text, the three truths the Spirit is actively convincing men of is _____, _____, and _____.

b) **Examples of His Ministry (Acts 2:37; 7:51; 9:5)**

1) Acts 2:37 - The example of _____

2) Acts 7:51 - The example of _____

3) Acts 9:5 - The example of _____

B. Regeneration

The impartation of _____ life to those who were dead (Ephesians 2:1-2).

1. Impartation

The regenerating work of the Spirit is the application of salvation in connection with the complete work of the _____ (Titus 3:2-7).

The regenerating work of the Spirit occurs at the same time as salvation.

2. Implications

a) **Regeneration makes the believer a new _____ (2 Corinthians 5:17).**

b) **Regeneration gives the believer _____ (1 John 2:20).**

C. Preservation (sealed)

1. Definition

This is the Work of the Spirit in salvation where the Spirit of God _____ us for eternity.

The preserving work of the Spirit occurs at the same time as salvation. This is an essential truth to the doctrine of _____ _____, which will be looked at in a future lesson.

2. Scripture

a) **Ephesians 1:13-14**

A "seal" was used to identify letters of importance. A wax was placed on the scroll and an impression was made on the wax which identified it. This seal was a mark of _____.

An "earnest" means a _____ _____ or promise.

b) **2 Corinthians 1:21-22**

In this text we again see the work of the Spirit is relation to the work of the Trinity in salvation.

School of Systematic Theology

    c)   **Ephesians 4:30**

        In this text we how the sealing of the Holy Spirit should affect our _____.

D. *Sanctification*

This is the work of the Spirit being involved in the _____ _____ or making _____ of the believer. This is related primarily to the position of the believer and the progress of their salvation.

1. The Spirit and Positional Sanctification

    a)   **2 Thessalonians 2:13**

        The Spirit is seen in connection with _____ in the Word of God in applying salvation to the sinner.

    b)   **1 Peter 1:2**

        The Spirit is seen once again working in conjunction the Trinity. It was the Father who _____ salvation, the Son who _____ salvation through His obedient sacrifice, and the Spirit is the one who _____ or applies it by setting the believer apart as God's own possession.

2. The Spirit and Progressive Sanctification

    a)   Romans 8:14 - The Spirit _____

    b)   Romans 8:16 - The Spirit _____

    c)   1 John 2:27 - The Spirit _____

    d)   John 14:16 - The Spirit _____

3. The Spirit and Perfected Sanctification

This is also called _____. The moment a believer dies we immediately complete the sanctification process as we receive our glorification.

    a)   **Romans 8:16-17**

        This verse explains that by virtue of being a _____ of God we will gain the same _____ of Jesus Christ. We will be glorified just as Jesus Christ was glorified.

    b)   **Romans 8:28-30**

        These verses show the progression of sanctification from

beginning to end.   First one is _____, because he was _____ and once called he was _____ and the final stage of justification is that he will be _____.

THOUGHT QUESTIONS FOR LESSON 7

1. Can the Spirit of God convict an individual of their sin apart from the Word of God? Explain your answer.

2. When someone says they are "born-again", what ministry of the Holy Spirit are they attributing their new life to?

3. A Christian friend tells you that if the Spirit is convicting someone of their sin, that individual cannot resist Him. Is this Christian right? What Scriptures would apply?

4. Another Christian friend tells you he has been saved three times now because he lost his salvation twice. What ministry of the Holy Spirit may help this young man understand the true nature of salvation? Give Bible verses.

5. Read Romans 8:9-17.
   - Write down any of the names given to the Spirit in this passage.
   - Write down any truths you find in this text about the Spirit.

Lesson 8:
God's Sovereignty and Man's Responsibility

The doctrine known as Calvinism is very popular among evangelicals. Most seem to think that a Christian must be either a Calvinist (believing in God's sovereignty) or Arminian (believing in human responsibility) in their view of salvation. This study is designed to examine these perspectives biblical.

I. God's Sovereignty (Calvinist Position)

Calvinism is a systematized doctrine developed by the followers of the 16th century Reformer, John Calvin. As a response to the doctrine of Arminianism, these individuals produced a system best known by its acronym _____. These five points were to reflect the beliefs of the man by whose name the system is known, John Calvin. These five points are intended to be understood and fit together; thus only a "five-point" Calvinist can legitimately say he is a Calvinist.

A. T_____ _____

1. The Explanation

This is an often-misunderstood term and probably more confusing than helpful. This term causes confusion because some think it means that man is as _____ as he could be and clearly not all people are as sinful as they could be. The idea of total depravity is that the _____ person was affected by the curse of sin. Therefore, our whole being is influence by our sin, including our _____. The question address here is the human will influenced by sin.

2. Scripture

a) **People are Born with Sin (a Sin Nature)**

(1) *Psalm 51:5*

(2) *Psalm 58:3*

(3) *Romans 5:12-19*

b) **People are Born Spiritual Dead**

(1) *Ephesians 2:1-3*

(2) *Colossians 2:13*

c) The Heart is Cursed by Sin
The heart in the Old Testament is the idea of the will.

(1) Jeremiah 17:9

(2) Titus 1:15

d) People are Slaves to Sin

(1) John 8:34

(2) Romans 6:16-20

B. U_____ _____

1. The Explanation
Unconditional election is the teaching that God has _____ those that will receive Him not influenced by anything they have done. This is an important doctrine to understand God is the author and finisher of man's salvation and that the work of man does not influence God's decision.

It must be remembered that God is eternal and outside of time. Therefore, when the Scripture talks about God elected men *"before the foundation of time"* (Ephesians 1:4), it must be understood that God is not bound by time. God is speaking to men to explain that God was in full control of the process of salvation, thus sovereign.

Unconditional election is God _____ _____. A misconception is that if God selected some to heaven then He must have therefore condemned other to hell. The understanding of total depravity reveals that hell is the destination of all humans. If God does not intervene then all people would rightly be sentenced to hell.

2. Scripture

a) Ephesians 1:3-6

b) Romans 9:10-24

c) Ephesians 2:10

d) Acts 13:48

e) Philippians 1:29

f) 1 Thessalonians 1:4-5

g) 2 Thessalonians 2:13-14

C. L_____ _____

1. The Explanation

Limited atonement is perhaps the most misconceived doctrine of the five. Some take this doctrine to mean that Christ's atoning work (his death on the cross) was a work performed only for the _____ and therefore salvation cannot be truly offered to the non-elect. However, the confusion is in the difference between the _____ of salvation (the gospel) and the _____ of salvation (the atonement or redemption).

The offer of salvation can be offered to all people but if there is even one person in hell than the application of salvation was _____. Limited atonement means that the application of the gospel is not applied to all people. It is therefore, not a universal atonement, meaning that all people will be saved. It deals with the application and not the offer.

The atonement addresses the redemption work of Jesus Christ as it is applied to the individual as payment for their sin.

2. Scripture

a) The Atoning Work of Jesus Christ

(1) 2 Corinthians 5:21

(2) Titus 2:14

(3) 1 Peter 3:18

(4) Romans 5:8-10

(5) 2 Corinthians 5:18-19

b) The Limited Work of Jesus Christ

(1) Matthew 1:21

(2) Matthew 20:28

(3) Matthew 26:28

(4) Hebrews 9:15, 28

D. I_____ _____

1. The Explanation

Irresistible grace is often explained in terms God redeeming a person first, either _____ or _____, and then the individual believing. This teaching is the core of much of the issue between the two views. The conflict is in an attempt to reconcile whose choice came first God's or man's. Some opponents teach that God somehow saves people against their will.

Though many acknowledge that a chronological ordering is wrong, they will create a logical order but still use chronological terminology, which creates confusion. This doctrine is best understood as _____ events. Thus, God works through the individual, such that, though the person chooses to believe, God worked through them so that the choice they made was as God intended it to be.

2. Scripture

a) Acts 16:14

b) John 3:8, 27

c) John 6:44

d) Romans 8:14

e) Philippians 2:12-13

f) 1 Corinthians 12:3

g) John 1:12-13

h) John 5:21

i) Ephesians 2:1-9

j) Philippians 1:29

k) Acts 18:27

l) 2 Timothy 2:25-26

m) 1 Corinthians 3:6-7

E. P_____ of the _____

  1. **The Explanation**

  The Bible clearly teaches that one who has truly received Christ as Lord and Savior and has demonstrated true repentance through spiritual fruit, will be saved _____. The fact is that if someone is saved they _____ have eternal life. It is _____ a future event. If one is genuinely saved and has accepted Christ as Lord and Savior, his salvation will be demonstrated in their life "unto the end" and they will be eternally saved. This is sometimes called the doctrine of eternal security, which will be discussed in the next lesson.

  2. **Scripture**

     a) Romans 5:8-10

     b) Romans 8:1, 29-30, 35-39

     c) John 3:16, 36

     d) John 5:24

     e) John 6:47

     f) 1 Corinthians 10:13

     g) 1 John 5:4, 11-13, 20

II. Human Responsibility (Arminianism Position)

A. *Commands to Repent and Believe*

Scripture is filled with commands to _____ and _____ for _____ people not just the elect. Repentance appears over 55 times in the New Testament. Man is commanded to repent and believe in order to be saved. Repentance is a human responsibility.

  1. **Acts 3:19**

  2. **Acts 17:30**

  3. **2 Peter 3:9**

  4. **Romans 10:9-10**

  5. **Mark 1:15**

6. **Mark 6:12**

7. **Matthew 3:2, 11**

B. *The Offer of Salvation is for All People*

Some people argue that the word "world" does not mean _____ people but some _____, specifically the elect. The clearest passage is 1 John 2:2, *"And He Himself is the propitiation for our sins, and not for ours only but also for the whole world"*. This verse states that Jesus is the _____ for our sins. That clearly means that Christ is the propitiation of the sins of all Christians, but the verse does not stop there. It continues to state that Jesus was the propitiation *"not for ours only but also the whole world"*.

There are three ways that reveal clearly that it means _____ person.

1) The use of the word *"world"* can mean every person based on context of the passage.

2) The word *"whole before world"* qualifies the meaning of the word *"world"* to refer to every person.

3) The comparison between the Christians and the world refers it to all non-Christians.

1. **John 1:29**

2. **John 3:16**

3. **John 6:51**

4. **2 Corinthians 5:19**

5. **1 Timothy 2:3-4**

6. **Isaiah 53:6**

C. *Whosoever Believes is Saved*

The Scriptures are clear that everyone that believes will be _____. Whosoever means _____ _____ _____, therefore it is _____. The gospel can be offered to all people because anyone that believes will be saved.

1. **Romans 10:4, 13**

2. **1 Timothy 4:10**

3. **1 John 5:1**

4. John 6:40

III. Reconciling Both Positions

The Scriptures teach that in the area of salvation God is sovereign and human's have a responsibility. How can both be true? Many think that these two positions must be mutually exclusive. However, we know from the doctrine of inspiration (which we will see in a later lesson on how we got the Bible) that God can work through a person so that the choices that the individual makes are exactly as God intends. The same is true for salvation. God chose us, outside of time and we chose God inside of time.

THOUGHT QUESTIONS FOR LESSON 8

1. A Calvinist says to you that the doctrine of election proves that you cannot choose God, He chooses you. How would you respond to him?

2. You hear a Calvinist declaring that no sinner can respond to salvation because he is spiritually dead. How would you address this illustration?

3. Read John 6:44. A Calvinist shows this to you as proof of the teaching of irresistible grace. How would you answer him?

4. An Arminianism tells you that you must believe in God before God can redeem you. How could you response?

5. Are the two views between God's sovereignty and human responsibility mutual exclusive. Explain your answer.

Lesson 9: Eternal Security

Are we always saved once we receive Jesus Christ as our Lord and Savior? What about people who say they are believers but have no fruit? Did they lose their salvation? These are some of the key questions being asked in Christianity today.

To the doctrine of eternal security there are a number of objections leveled. This lesson intends to address the objections to this doctrine as well as provide Scriptural evidence for the doctrine of Eternal Security.

"Eternal security" is a phrase not found in Scripture, yet the concept is a clear teaching. This concept may be defined as "the belief that once a person enters into a relationship with God, they may never lose that relationship." (The following study adapted from Doug Bookman's work on the subject).

I. FALSE VIEWS OF ETERNAL SECURITY

There are two false views which are prominent concerning the permanence of salvation.

    A. *The View of the _____ _____*

        1. They believe that salvation may be _____ by the committing of _____ sin.

        2. Salvation may also be _____ by the authority of the _____.

        3. This belief makes salvation ultimately dependent upon the _____.

    B. The _____ Position

        1. A person may only be assured that they have salvation in the _____.

        2. A person may lose their salvation if they fall into willful _____ or _____.

        3. This belief makes the assurance of salvation dependent upon the _____.

4. Who believes in this view of security?

   a) _____

   b) _____

   c) _____

   d) _____

II. BIBLICAL VIEW OF ETERNAL SECURITY

A. Definition
God _____ and _____ final salvation for all true believers. The importance of this truth is that this recognizes God as the _____ of salvation; not the church and not the individual.

B. Defense
Below is a list of a number of direct statements from Scripture which present a defense for the biblical doctrine of eternal security.

1. John 6:39 –

2. John 10:27-30 -

3. Romans 8:31-39 -

4. Romans 11:29 -

5. 1 Corinthians 1:8-9 -

6. Ephesians 4:30 -

7. Philippians 1:6 -

8. 1 Thessalonians 5:23-24 -

9. 2 Thessalonians 3:3 -

C. Doctrines

There are a number of related doctrines which also reinforce the doctrine of eternal security.

1. **The priestly ministry of Jesus (John 17:24; Hebrews 7:25)**

2. **The sealing ministry of the Spirit (Ephesians 1:13; 4:30)**

3. **The purpose of God in salvation (1 Peter 1:5; Romans 8:1)**

4. **The union of the believer with Christ (Colossians 3:3)**

D. Difficulties

There are a number of objections which the opponent of the doctrine of eternal security presents which must be addressed.

1. **What about passages which speak of the Lord rejecting those who thought they were saved?**

    a) The Scriptures

    (1) Matthew 7:21-23

    (2) 2 Peter 2:20-21

    (3) John 6:63-66

    b) The Explanation
    These are passages which address _____ believers and NOT _____ believers. These people would be considered _____ converts.

2. **Will not the doctrine of eternal security encourage people to sin?**

    a) This is an argument from _____.

    b) The Explanation
    Salvation does not mean we have been freed to sin, it means that we have been freed from sin (Romans 6:15-22; Galatians 5:1; 13). Any believer who teaches license to sin does not understand salvation.

School of Systematic Theology

3. **How about the unpardonable sin?**

   a) The Scripture - Matthew 12:43-45

   b) **The Explanation**
   First, it must be understood that the unpardonable sin was _____ committed by a professing believer. Second, this is the only occurrence we have of the unpardonable sin. We understand the unpardonable sin to be the observing of the works of Christ personally, and attributing them to Satan.

4. **What about those passages which talk about Christian leaders who fell away from the truth?**

   a) **The Scriptures**

   (1) *Acts 20:29-30*

   (2) *2 Timothy 4:10*

   (3) *2 Timothy 4:14*

   b) **The Explanation**
   These passages speak of _____ religious leaders who crept into the true church and spread their false doctrine. These were never said to be true believers.

5. **Are there not verses which say a believer may lose their salvation?**

   a) **The Scriptures**

   (1) *Hebrews 6:4-6*

   (2) *James 5:19-20*

   (3) *1 John 5:16-17*

   (4) *Galatians 5:4*

   b) **The Explanation**
   These passages either address the believer's loss of _____ or are describing those who have heard the gospel and are either attempting another means of salvation (Galatians 5:4), or are rejecting the truth (Hebrews 6:4-6?).

6. **How about those verses which teach that an individual may lose the Holy Spirit?**

   a) **The Scriptures**

      (1) 1 Samuel 16:14

      (2) Psalm 51:8-12

   b) **The Explanation**
   Individuals who cite these verses misunderstand the ministry of the Holy Spirit in the Old Testament. Indwelling of the Holy Spirit is a ministry of the Spirit since the inception of the church, not in the Old Testament. These are references not to salvation but to the _____ of the individual.

THOUGHT QUESTIONS FOR LESSON 9

1. What are some of the practical merits of the biblical doctrine of eternal security?

2. Read Hebrews 6:4-6. If this was talking about someone losing their salvation (and it is not), what else would be true about that individual? How does this affect the salvation doctrine of the Pentecostals?

3. An individual says to you that they have committed the unpardonable sin. How would you answer this person?

4. Read Matthew 18:15-19. Why do you think Jesus says to treat this individual as a sinner? Does this mean he lost his salvation? Explain your answer.

Lesson 10:
The Blessings of Salvation

Very few Christians contemplate the blessings which are theirs at salvation. For some, the only blessing is eternal life. For others, the blessing of salvation is solely what God can now do for them.

This study provides the student with the many blessings that the Christian receives at the moment of salvation.

I. WE ARE SANCTIFIED

There are basically three ideas that we mean when we discuss being sanctified. The first is _____ sanctification, the second is _____ sanctification and the last is _____ sanctification.

A. Positional Sanctification

1. **Definition**

    The reality that at the moment of our salvation we were _____ _____ by God as objects of His ownership. This means that we have been removed from the _____ of sin.

2. **Scripture**

    a) 1 Corinthians 6:11

    b) Hebrews 10:10, 14

B. Progressive Sanctification

1. **Definition**

    The fact that an individual who has been positionally set apart by God will progress in becoming more like Christ. This means that we have been delivered from the _____ of sin.

2. **Scripture**

    a) 1 Peter 1:14-15

    b) John 12:17

    c) 2 Peter 3:18

C. Perfected Sanctification

1. **Definition**

   The fact that the believer will be ultimately and totally separate from sin and with God for eternity. This speaks of our deliverance from the _____ of sin.

2. **Scripture**

   a) 1 Thessalonians 3:12-13

   b) 1 John 3:2

II. WE ARE UNITED WITH CHRIST

This reality is associated with the spiritual _____ that occurred at our salvation (see 1 Corinthians 12:13).

While there is no comprehensible way to define specifically this union, a description of this union noting the nature of our union with Christ and the Need for our union with Christ will help us in our understanding.

A. The Nature of Our Union with Christ

1. It is a _____ union (John 14:23)

2. It is a _____ union (1 John 5:11-12)

3. It is an _____ union (Roman 8:38-39)

4. It is a _____ union (Colossians 1:26-27)

B. The Need of Our Union with Christ

Our union with Christ is the _____ of all spiritual blessings (Ephesians 1:3-13)

1. **Essential for _____ of Christ** (Galatians 2:20; Romans 6:4; Ephesians 2:6)

2. **Essential for _____ in Christ** (John 14:13; Romans 8:2; 1 Corinthians 1:30; 1 Thessalonians 4:16)

3. **Essential for _____ with Christians** (Galatians 3:28; 1 Corinthians 12:13)

III. WE ARE JUSTIFIED

A. Significance
Justification is the judicial act of God where He _____ and not _____ the believer righteous before Himself. The basis of justification is the believer's union with Christ.

B. Summary
Doug Bookman reduced the teaching of the doctrine of justification to the following summary:

1. **The SOURCE of Justification (Romans 3:24) -** _____

2. **The BASIS of Justification (Romans 5:9) -** _____

3. **The APPROPRIATION of Justification (Romans 3:28) -** _____

4. **The EVIDENCE of Justification (James 2:24) -** _____ _____

IV. WE HAVE BEEN _____

Adoption is the act of God, Who places the believer into His family at conversion.

To fully appreciate this doctrine, we need to understand the background and examine the blessings of adoption.

A. Background of Adoption
The concept is taken from the Greco-Roman idea of adoption of a child by parents who were childless. By Roman law, these adopted children were entitled to everything natural children were, even if the parents of adopted children had natural children as well; equal benefits, equal inheritance, equal in all things.

B. Basis of Adoption

1. The _____ of God (Ephesians 1:5)

2. The _____ of Christ (Galatians 4:4-5)

C. Benefits of Adoption

1. We are placed into a family in which we did not previously belong (Ephesians 2:3)

2. We have all the rights and privileges of being in God's family (Romans 8:15; cf. 1 Peter 1:4)

3. We are promised full adoption when we are home with our heavenly Father (Romans 8:23)

V. WE ARE PROVIDED ACCESS TO GOD

This doctrine speaks of the _____ of the believer, the fact that God has provided each believer access into His presence (1 Peter 2:9).

A. The Basis of this Access - God's Grace (Romans 5:2)

B. The Blessing of this Access - Help in time of need (Hebrews 4:16)

C. The Boldness of this Access - Our relationship with Him (Hebrews 4:15-16; 10:19-20)

THOUGHT QUESTIONS FOR LESSON 10

1. Because of these truths, what are some things you will thank God for in your private time?

2. A fellow believer does not understand what the word "sanctification" means. Explain to him this doctrine and try not to look back in your notes.

3. Read 1 Peter 1:4-5. How is our inheritance described? Who is the one who keeps our inheritance?

4. Read 1 Peter 2:9. What are the four descriptions of the believer in this verse? What is the significance of each?

Bibliography

Boice, James M. Foundations of the Christian Faith. Downers Grove, Ill.: InterVarsity Press, 1986.

Bookman, Douglas. Unpublished Class Notes on Man, Sin, and Salvation. Minnesota: Pillsbury Baptist Bible College, 1983.

Chafer, Lewis Sperry. Salvation. Grand Rapids: Zondervan Publishing, 1955.

Five Views of Sanctification. Grand Rapids: Zondervan Publishing, 1987.

Good, Kenneth H. Are Baptist Calvinist? Oberlin, OH: Regular Baptist Heritage Fellowship, 1975.

Ironside, H.A. Holiness: The False and the True. Neptune, NJ: Loizeaux Brothers, Inc., 1912.

MacArthur, John. The Gospel According to Jesus. Grand Rapids: Zondervan Publishing, 1988.

Mueller, Marc. Unpublished Class Notes on Soteriology. Sun Valley, CA.: The Master's Seminary, 1988.

Ryrie, Charles. Basic Theology. Wheaton, Ill.: Victor Books, 1987.

_____. So Great Salvation. Wheaton, Ill.: Victor Books, 1989.

Shank, William. Elect in the Son. Springfield, MO: Wescott Publishers, 1970.

www.ingramcontent.com/pod-product-compliance
Lightning Source LLC
Chambersburg PA
CBHW081206170426
43197CB00018B/2936